Shattering the Illusions (for Teens and Young Adults)

10 Truths About Adulthood That You Should Know

PAM SMITH

Shattering the Illusions (for Teens and Young Adults). Copyright 2021 by Pam Smith. All rights reserved. No part of this publication may be reproduced, distributed, or transmitted in any form or by any means, including photocopying, recording, or other electronic or mechanical methods, without the prior written permission of the publisher, except in the case of brief quotations embodied in critical reviews and certain other noncommercial uses permitted by copyright law.

For permission requests, write to the publisher, addressed "Attention: Permissions Coordinator," 205 N. Michigan Avenue, Suite #810, Chicago, IL 60601. 13th & Joan books may be purchased for educational, business or sales promotional use. For information, please email the Sales Department at sales@13thandjoan.com.

Printed in the U. S. A.

First Printing, December 2021.

Library of Congress Cataloging-in-Publication Data has been applied for.

ISBN: 978-1-953156-58-7

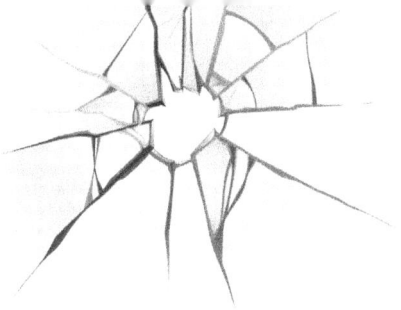

DEDICATION

For Zaire, Hakim, and Londyn

"Not many of you should become teachers, my fellow believers, because you know that we who teach will be judged more strictly."
James 3:1

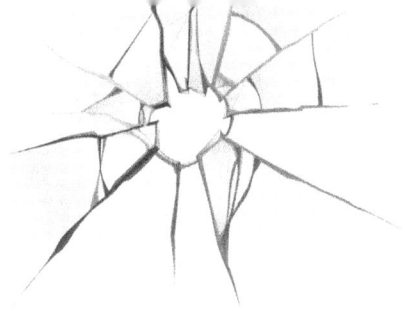

PREFACE

THE PURPOSE OF this book is to be really honest with teens and young adults about life and what's ahead. I remember wishing I had some real guidance at times, but not from my friends, parents or teachers, because they all had their own opinions so I surely got different answers. I wanted guidance from someone who was neutral to level with me since my choices had no effect on them at all. I did get some advice in the military, but I was a soldier so every decision made at the time was based on how it could possibly affect my military career. Throughout the years as I worked, I met many different people from ages 20 through 60, and I would always hear the same thing, "I wish someone was around to tell me the truth." They each shared with me that there was a point in life when they wished someone had kept it real with them.

Well this is me keeping it real with you. This is me shattering the illusions for you. The illusion that when you're grown everything falls into place. There is no miraculous download of information to come. Your whole life you've probably heard things like, "you'll understand when you're older," or, "wait until you're an adult." The truth is, adults have painted the fallacy that life gets easier once you become an adult. Let's use the analogy of bowling. In bowling, we allow the inexperienced players to use the bumpers. The bumpers keep the ball in the lane and from going into the gutter. They guarantee that you will hit a pin. It may not be a strike but it's certain that you won't miss. Once you become an adult, the bumpers are removed. Removing the bumpers forces you to be more cautious and to strategize your aim towards your target. The chance of your ball going into the gutter has increased greatly. As you continue to play and you become a more experienced bowler, your skills improve resulting in more strikes. The ball may go into the gutter once in a while, but you figure it out. Well...THAT'S LIFE! Life is bowling without the bumpers.

In each truth we will discuss the illusion and the truth behind it. I have also added some suggested advice that you may or may not use depending on how you see fit. Take what works for you or don't take any at all. It is 100% your choice and you are under no obligation to do so. In the last section of each chapter I include my personal experiences of dealing with the illusion. The chapters end with a reflection page. I encourage you to reflect on what you read, take notes, and shatter illusions in your own life.

While the truths are presented in numerical order, you can read them however you would like. The chapters can be read independently. So you can begin reading in the middle of the book or even in the last chapter. I hope you find this book helpful. My truths are meant to be insightful yet entertaining.

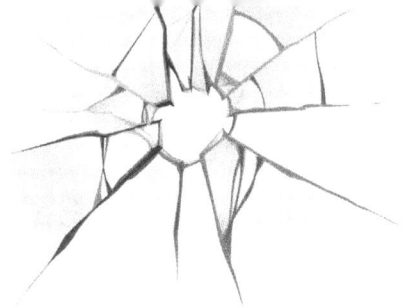

TABLE OF CONTENTS

Preface v
Truth #1 High School Is an Illusion................... 1
    My Illusion..................................... 6
    Truth Check-in 9
Truth #2 College is NOT for Everyone................. 11
    My Illusion.................................... 17
    Truth Check-in 20
Truth #3 Adults F#% Up Too! 21
    My Illusion.................................... 25
    Truth Check-in 28
Truth #4 Our Fear Can Hold Us Back.................. 29
    My Illusion.................................... 32
    Truth Check-in 36
Truth #5 The Choices You Make Now Can Affect You
    Forever 37
    My Illusion.................................... 42
    Truth Check-in 45

Truth #6 Sex ≠≠ Love; It's Just Sex 47
    My Illusion.................................. 50
    Truth Check-in 55
Truth #7 We Allow Others To Put Limits on Us 57
    My Illusion.................................. 61
    Truth Check-in 64
Truth #8 We All Have Dreams 65
    My Illusion.................................. 73
    Truth Check-in 79
Truth #9 Financial Literacy 81
    My Illusion.................................. 90
    Truth Check-in 94
Truth #10 Live In the Moment 95
    My Illusion.................................. 104
    Truth Check-in 109
    References 113

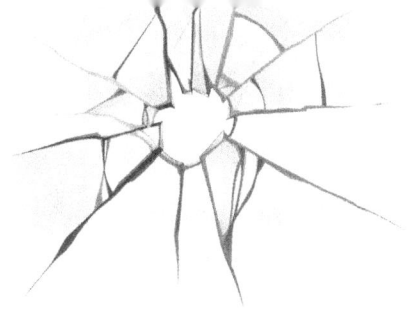

TRUTH #1
HIGH SCHOOL IS AN ILLUSION

IMAGINE THIS, IT is the end of your Junior year of high school and as you figure out how you plan to spend the summer, you reflect on school. Your grades are in pretty good shape, you have a great group of friends, and you have managed to keep your parents and teachers off your back. Senior year is bound to be epic! Right? Fast forward to the first day of senior year. There is excitement everywhere. Everyone's buzzing around trying to find their classes and lockers. Teachers welcome you back to school and congratulate you on being a senior. Walking through the halls, you can hear conversations about summer vacation and expectations for the school year. In homeroom you are greeted with hugs and high fives from smiling familiar faces. You join your friends' conversation about life after high school. Most are going to college, some are moving away with family, and a few others have decided to join the military. There is a small group of students that have no clue what they are doing after high school. You then realize that you too fall into the group of the clueless. Suddenly the nerves kick in. As you begin to think about what you're gonna do after graduation, senior year begins to look a bit scary. You haven't really thought about it, but all your friends seem so sure of their futures. You think to yourself, "how am I not ready? I made it to senior year and did everything I was told to do."

Your parents and teachers have probably been talking to you about your future plans, right? I bet you thought that you had time or that you would just know when the time was right. Well time moves fast. If you had not thought much about the future, then senior year will surely catch you off guard. The time you had is now gone and you might not be so sure of just knowing. The good thing is that it is never too late to start planning for the future. So let's talk about it.

Truth:

High school is an illusion. No one is ready for life after high school. High school is its own alternate world and it is like nothing else. It does not represent real life at all. The past 15 years of school have only prepared you for the next grade. Kindergarten prepared you for 1st grade. 5th grade prepared you for middle school, which prepared you for high school. That is where the preparation stops. You are now expected to know everything you need to know. Honestly no one can be fully prepared for anything. There will always be situations that you can't plan for.

If you played a sport or participated in a club then you have a little more preparation. A sport or club teaches you responsibility and accountability because you agree to the requirements of the group. You are then assigned a task or position that you are expected to perform. When you don't uphold your obligation you are held accountable for your actions. Therefore you must accept the consequences as a result. Participating in these types of groups also teaches you about working with others. As you enter college and the workforce, you will have to work with different people as a team to get things accomplished. Like sports, everyone has a task to perform and their contribution is just as important as yours. You might not get along with all your teammates but you need to figure out how to work together to complete the goal. This is how participating in other activities in high school will help your transition into adulthood.

Advice:
Take learning in your own hands as you approach adulthood. Spend the summers touring local college campuses. This includes technical and community colleges, trade schools and training programs. During your visit,

speak with students, teachers and staff to understand their environment and expectations. If there is not an official tour provided by the college, then visit the admissions office and introduce yourself, then ask to speak with an advisor as a prospective student.

You can spend a summer or two working. Get a job or work in the family business. This is an excellent way to experience what is really taking place in the real world. It also helps to build your responsibility muscle. Working builds transferable skills, like communication, time-management, and responsibility. Indeed.com defines transferable skills as qualities that can be transferred from one job to another, meaning that skills that you've learned on one job can be used at another job.

You can volunteer. Volunteering is a great way to gain knowledge and experience. There are many organizations in your community that need volunteers. They want to share their cause. Also organizations love when young people take interest. They are eager to mentor and guide future leaders.

Job Shadowing is another way you can explore career opportunities. If you think you're interested in a career but you don't know much about it, you can reach out to an employer and schedule a job shadow opportunity. If you cannot job shadow, ask to tour the facility and conduct an informational interview. If you are interested in the technology field, try watching YouTube videos to gain insight on the various tech careers. Research company websites to learn what services they offer and to gain access to an email list of managers. Then send an introduction email explaining that you're a graduating student and you'd like to ask a few questions about career areas, and asking if they are able to schedule you for a quick call.

Remember that when asking for a tour or informational call, these are actual work environments, so be mindful of their time. Arrive or make the call at the allotted time.

Also, taking any of this advice can be intimidating, so it is okay to ask your parents, teachers, or counselors for help.

MY ILLUSION

In high school, I was average. My high school did not have a huge student body, but it was big enough. With just under 1,000 students, I could still go unnoticed. I wasn't popular, I was just kinda there. Jones High School students' were majority Black and located right in the middle of Central Florida. My grades were pretty good, but so were everyone else's. In my eyes, Jones bred that kind of excellence. The captain and co-captain of the cheerleading squad were also the Valedictorian and Salutatorian. The players of the football team also held offices in the Student Government, National Honor Society, and as future business leaders. My illusion was that I was not excellent. I compared myself to others, which is not a good thing and NEVER accurate. I felt invisible. I felt trapped and knew that I had to get away. Hometowns can be like that. No matter how big they are, they can still feel small. I didn't have plans for after high school. I had not spoken to anyone about career paths. I had not visited or applied for any colleges. I had no direction, but I knew I needed to do something.

I was raised by my grandmother who was very old fashioned and she had already planned my future to her liking. Her exact plan was for me to attend the local community college and enroll into some kind of medical program like CNA or nursing. She had already retired as a physical therapist aide. I would continue to work at my job and come home at night to be in the house with her. Yikes!!! Talk about suffocating! I did not know what I wanted to do with my life but THAT certainly was not it! So I had to figure something out or else I'd be forever lost in the illusion.

I remembered the times the military recruiters had come to the school. At that time, Orlando, Florida had one of the biggest naval training bases for new recruits. So I joined the United States Navy. I served 4 years and it did exactly what I needed it to do. It shattered the illusion. The bullying that I experienced as a kid and the invisibility of high school was replaced with strength and confidence that I learned as a soldier. The Navy gave me confidence and they taught me that I was stronger than I knew. I developed transferable skills such as: teamwork, problem solving, and increased attention to detail, not to mention the two very important skills: independence and survival.

"Each one should test their own actions.
Then they can take pride in themselves alone, without comparing themselves to someone else."
(Galatians 6:4)

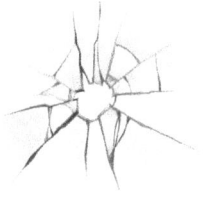

TRUTH CHECK-IN

Use this sheet to keep track of the colleges, programs and your areas of interest.

Name of School/ Business	Person of Contact Name/Phone/ Email	Area of Interest	Notes

Name of School/ Business	Person of Contact Name/Phone/ Email	Area of Interest	Notes

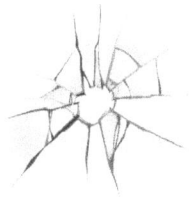

TRUTH #2
COLLEGE IS NOT FOR EVERYONE

THE ALLURE OF college is exciting. In the movies and on television, there are pretty girls, hot boys, and parties. On an HBCU campus, they all look so glamorous and fine. The activism and student unions keep you informed and involved. Let's not forget the sports! College football games, basketball games, and baseball games will engage you and leave you wanting more. College looks like a lot of fun and it is, but it is also a lot of work. You must have a certain level of discipline to attend college. You are adults now and will be treated as such. It will be your responsibility to remember due dates for your assignments. Unlike high school, attending classroom lectures will not be enough, you will have to take notes. If you hardly ever study, then you will have to develop better study habits. You will have to manage your time to accommodate your schedule and dedicate personal time outside of class to your studies. That means possibly missing out on a party, game, or hanging with your friends. Be ready to hold yourself accountable for getting your college education. Some online colleges are even more rigorous because you don't physically attend campus. By now you're probably feeling the pressure about college. You have had conversations with adults telling you how important going to college is to your success, but here's the tea....college is not for everyone.

Truth:

The illusion that you need a college degree to be successful is simply not true. In Truth #1 we discussed how high school does little to prepare you for real life, but the truth is that having a degree is no guarantee that you will be successful. Yes a degree will qualify you for opportunities that a High School Diploma will not, however, if you are not disciplined enough to handle the responsibility of college then you won't have a good experience. This is not to say that you should never go to college. Some students attend college a little later once they have become a bit more disciplined and responsible.

Some would have you believe that going to college is your next best step, but if you have never been on your own then going to college is scary. You could end up worrying about all the other things going on, that you couldn't focus in class. If your parents cannot support you financially while you're at college, then what will you do? Have you had a job? Do you know how to get a job? What about paying bills? I am not trying to scare you. My intent is to show you the level of responsibility you need to have for college. Remember, you are still expected to attend class and complete assignments. College can be fun, but it takes discipline and a lot of hard work.

When I was in junior high school (7th, 8th and 9th grade), we had elective classes. In elementary, we were just assigned to go to music or art class. However in junior high, we got to pick our electives based on our interest since they were not core classes. There were still classes like art and music, although music was more like joining the marching band or choir. Junior high school offered more areas of interest such as: drafting, photography, wood shop, and home economics. Living in Florida also meant that we had agriculture classes too that taught us about farming and resources that were a natural part of our surroundings. These types of classes have since been removed as schools moved more towards a college focused curriculum. However, it is these types of career exploration programs that I feel are still needed.

In 2020 you witnessed many people lose their jobs when the pandemic shut down the world. You saw people who were frightened and worried about how they were going to take care of their families. Now let me tell you what I saw. I saw people become completely reliant on the essential worker. Reliant on positions that previously were less desirable. Cashiers, delivery drivers, construction workers, jobs that do not require a college education suddenly became essential. I say these positions have ALWAYS been essential. I saw these people continue to earn an income while everyone else was trying to get unemployment and stimulus checks. There was a special appreciation for teachers, who ironically have to earn a college degree, but still are paid low wages. Front line medical workers were praised and celebrated for their sacrifice as well. Yet a lot of these people are making minimum wage. Does that seem fair? Do you know what else I saw? I saw some people who were not able to pivot; besides their college education, they had no technical skill or trade that they could use to earn a living while they were on furlough. What would *you* have done?

Advice:

If going to college is not a part of the future that you see for yourself at this time, there are other avenues available to gain additional education and training. Trade and technical schools as well as apprenticeship programs are great alternatives. You can earn a certification for specific job fields. Enlisting in the military is another option too. If you are already working, there are some companies that offer their own "in-house" training, such as a leadership development track for employees who desire to advance within the company. For entrepreneurs wanting to start your own business, try contacting the Small Business Association. They have mentors who are willing to coach and assist you with getting started. Don't overlook your local non-profits either. They have career advisors who have access to job training programs and partnerships. They can also help you determine which career fields interest you. Or you can do this for yourself by taking a free online career assessment. There are no right or wrong answers. This is only to help you find your career interests. Mynextmove.org has one of my personal favorite assessments. Truity.com has an awesome Photo Career assessment, where you select jobs from a series of pictures. These are just a couple, but there are many other career assessments. So have fun with them and maybe you will discover something new about yourself!

Let's assume that your goal is to become a professional athlete. There have been very few candidates that didn't play at a collegiate level before entering professional sports. As a college and then professional athlete, your body is your instrument. It is therefore your responsibility to care for your body and keep it in optimal condition. Like any other profession, you maintain and keep equipment in prime working condition. A race car driver will keep his car tuned up and running. A chef will keep her knives and cooking equipment ready for service. Pilots expect for their airplanes to be inspected and maintained by operating standards. So for an athlete, your body is that machine and your responsibility. If you research some of the top performing athletes you will see that they have very disciplined regimens. Basketball greats like Michael Jordan, Kobe Bryant, and Lebron James, heavyweight boxer Floyd Mayweather and tennis champion Serena Williams, all established a combination of diet, training, and rest to keep their bodies performance ready. We never see Beyoncé yelling or screaming because her voice is her instrument so she does not put extra strain on it. Singers must allow adequate rest of their vocal cords. Certain sacrifices are necessary for your career. You may have to limit your social activities and eliminate late night partying. I suggest you refrain from drug use of any kind and limit the consumption of alcohol. If you are going to do it, then take your career seriously enough to protect your instrument.

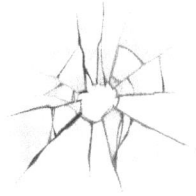

MY ILLUSION

As graduation approached, I was not sure of what path to take. The obvious path was laid out in front of me. I was in the top 10% of my graduating class, so we had all earned scholarships to the local community college. My grandma was way too happy about the scholarship because this provided a reason for me to remain at home after graduation. However, I did not want to go to college. I was over school! College was not for me. I was over being home too, and the military looked like my best move at the time.

The Navy taught me some very important life skills. Like sports, teamwork is the foundation of the military and you are in it together. A mistake could lose the championship or get someone hurt. However, responsibility in the military is next level. You are responsible for your safety and your teams' safety as well as. A wrong move or miscalculation can result in more fatal consequences.

One of the main characteristics I developed was work ethic. In the military, laziness is not an option. You must perform to your maximum potential at all times and are expected to do so. Regardless of rain, snow, or whatever. You will report to duty. I also learned to be independent and make decisions for myself.

Four years later, after leaving the Navy and entering the workforce, I found that not all of my military training could translate into civilian life. Some of my skills were specifically for being on a ship. I needed additional education to accompany my training. I enrolled in a program and earned my certification to make me more competitive in the job market. Honestly, I did not attend college until I was much older. I had tried different programs, so I was determined to complete something. I realized that I still felt the same way about college but my motivation for going was different. Here is some extra advice: whatever career you choose, make sure it is what *you* want to do. DO NOT pick a career only for money or solely because your parents want you to. Please have some interest in the career. This will make all the difference if you complete the training or find the job worth it. So many people spend time earning a degree or certification that they will never use because it turns out they don't like the field. Which is why Truth #1 would be beneficial for you.

"Do not conform to the pattern of this world, but be transformed
by the renewing of your mind.
Then you will be able to test and approve what God's will is..."
(Roman 12:2)

TRUTH CHECK-IN

What other paths are you considering
in addition to college?

_____

_____

_____

_____

_____

_____

_____

_____

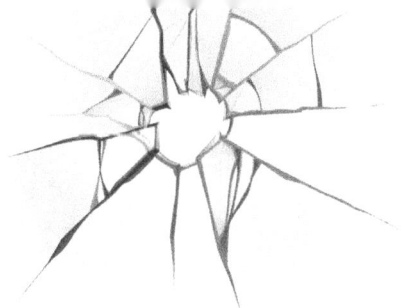

TRUTH #3
ADULTS F#% UP TOO!

"**B**ECAUSE I SAID so." "I've already been where you are trying to go." You have probably heard either of these statements before. These are the things adults say when they are pulling rank over young people. Have you had suspicions that maybe they don't know or can't find the answer? Or maybe they know, but they don't tell you the truth because they say they are trying to protect you? Parents tell their children that they wouldn't let anything happen to them, so nothing ever does. In this case that is a good thing. If you have gone your whole childhood and did not know your parents were struggling, then they did their job. If you never knew if a bill was past due, if you always had heat, running water and electricity, then they did their job. Have you ever been homeless? Did you have presents at Christmas? Then stop what you're doing and thank your parents. I say this because sometimes sh@t happens right in the middle of life! On the flip side, if you are like me and have had a couple of these experiences, you should *still* thank your parents! They are doing the best they can with what they have. The adults in your life are doing their best to not burden you with grown up issues. However, some adults do not do a good job at this. Some teens can end up parenting the adults and that is a lot of pressure. Perhaps you've had to help raise younger brothers and sisters? Imagine having to drop out of school because you are needed to assume the adult role in your home. That is like a junior varsity player moving to the varsity team before they are ready. Sure they know the basics and can play the position, but they have not developed the skill and maturity it takes to play against the other varsity teams. To be honest, some adults just don't have their stuff together. They have not developed their own adulting skills, yet they are raising young adults.

Although it may not seem like it, life moves fast and at times we are not ready for what comes in. Remember we thought that we had time. When we have not learned the skills that we need then we can end up not being the best role models to our children. At one time, role models were limited to our parents, teachers, or people in our community. Sometimes people or characters we saw on TV programs. Now we have more access to each other's lives than ever before. Our actions and mistakes are a lot more visible and this visibility contributes to the need to appear perfect.

Truth:

The truth is, adults are scared that they may not know how to help you. They do know a lot but not everything. Some of them became parents at the same age you are now. Like you, they were just trying to figure life out. To a young child, adults seem like they have all the answers. It is easy to give simple answers or divert the questions of a 9 year old. However as you grow, the questions become more complex and answers are more gray and less black and white. Teens ask questions that make adults uncomfortable because you are coming into adulthood yourself. Do parents, teachers, and siblings seem less knowledgeable now? All of a sudden they don't have the answers because some things you learn as you go. Parenting included. This is especially so for first born children, everything is new to them so they don't know what to really expect. Generationally speaking, you're having experiences as a teen that your parents and even grandparents did not have. Just think about how technology has advanced since you were younger.

Back in the 90s, pagers and flip phones were the leading modes of communication. If you had a sidekick or the version of pager where you could send messages and not just numbers, well then you were way ahead. The only way to play your friends in a video game was to go to their house. Thanks to the internet we have access to people from around the globe. Smart phones and video game systems allow us to play with others and never leave our homes. It is this same access that puts our lives on display. Everyone can see our decisions in real time. Be honest, do you want your life to be on display all the time? Still our mistakes are broadcasted and we are instantly judged. We are not given the time to self assess, and rarely do we see remorse and acts of redemption.

Advice:

Not all adults (parents included) have it all together, so try to be understanding regarding their pressures. They are learning how to be parents and still learning themselves. Let's be real for a minute and talk about the characteristics of people. Some people are not nice. They are mean bullies. While some people are too nice. They won't stand up for themselves. They allow others to take advantage of them or take them for granted. Some people only want peace. Still there are others who stand up for what's right. Etc. Everyone is finding their way. So what happens to these characteristics when people become parents? Nothing. They are still those people with the same character traits, values and views, except they have children now. Be it good or bad, some of those values get taught to their children. You.

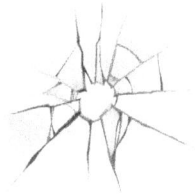

MY ILLUSION

I was raised by my grandmother. She was very hardworking and did the best she could. I know I made it difficult at times but I was a teen. I had tunnel vision and was caught up in the illusion, and dealing with my feelings. I did not consider what my grandmother was going through. It is hard for Black people to talk about grief even though it is a crucial part of the grieving process. My mom died when I was 12 (two days before my 13th birthday to be exact). She was 38 years old and she was an alcoholic. When she drank, she wasn't mean or anything like that. She was just drunk all the time. My mom battled with alcoholism to the point where she couldn't work or raise her kids (me and my older brother). I lived with my grandmother my whole life. My mom was not capable of taking care of us. My dad had a new family so she wasn't his problem. I can remember being at the neighborhood store with friends and my mom would come in...drunk. She came staggering in. She slurred her words as she spoke and smelled like she hadn't bathed in a couple of days. Her clothes were dirty and stained from where she had peed on herself, which was something she did a lot and I had witnessed for myself. One of my friends asked, "is that your mom?" I said, "yeah," and walked out the store. I was so embarrassed. She drank so much that she would get sick. She threw up all over the place. Her hands shook so badly that she could not hold a glass of water. Once my grandmother told me a story about how one day when I was in the care of my mom, she dropped me off at a daycare. My brother was already old enough to go to school. This was not my normal daycare, just some random place because she no longer wanted to watch me. The issue was that she forgot to come back for me. I was apparently old enough to have learned my phone number, but the daycare worker had to wait until after working hours for my grandmother to be home to answer the phone. She had to drive to the other side of town to pick me up.

Later after I became an adult and had kids of my own, I realized that adults don't know everything. We f#% up too. We are just trying to figure it out. Unfortunately some of us have children long before we have a grasp over our own lives. My mom was an addict. When she had us that didn't stop it, she just became an addict with kids. I didn't understand that. I was angry and placed a lot of blame on her, but addiction is a demon of its own. I am forever grateful to my grandmother. She did the best she could to preserve my childhood.

"After all, children should not have to save up for their parents, but parents for their children."
(2 Corithians 12:14)

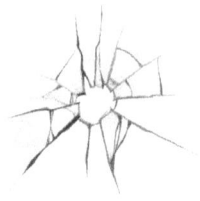

TRUTH CHECK-IN

Think of an experience where possibly a parent/adult was having difficulty. What can you do next time to handle it better?

_____

_____

_____

_____

_____

_____

_____

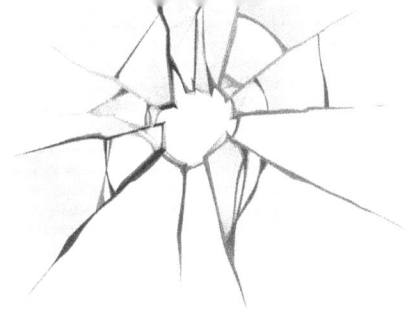

TRUTH #4
OUR FEAR CAN HOLD US BACK

"**I'M DOING THIS** for your own good." I bet you heard this multiple times. Sometimes that is accurate and other times it is not. For the times that it is not, this is really what is going on....

Fear is one of the main motivating factors of life. Whether we are afraid for ourselves or afraid for others, it influences our choices. Have you ever kept a secret or held something back out of fear of what would happen? Did you break a window or lamp while playing ball or hit something when driving but you pretended that you didn't know anything about it? You were fearful of the repercussions right? Maybe your friends were making plans that you knew were risky but you did it anyway. Why would you put yourself in danger? Are you afraid that they won't see you as cool and that you would lose them? You see, fear can show up on all levels. Most people hear the word fear and think of some BIG obstacle, but fear can be as small and subtle as walking into class on the first day of school. Either way it still influences our actions and responses to situations.

Truth:

The truth is that we are all scared. Our own experiences definitely influence the guidance we as adults give you. If we have bad experiences then our fear will cause us to want to protect you from experiencing what we have. The problem with that is we end up protecting you from *all* experiences. We think the worst in everything. We will say that we are scared for you, but we are really scared for ourselves. Scared that we cannot protect you. Scared that the help you'd need would be outside of our capabilities. On the flip side, if our experiences have been pleasant and only mildly dangerous, then we can push you out of YOUR comfort zone. We can disrupt the foundation that you are developing as a young adult. You have your own intuition that you need to learn to trust. If you are pushed too fast then it can accelerate your fear and anxiety.

In Truth #3, we talked about how technology has changed. How you now have access to anyone anywhere at any time. For parents, that is a scary thought. It used to be that we only had to worry about physical threats. Predators or bullies had to physically engage you and we could intercept most of that. Now imagine having to block in all directions. Technology and the internet has created many avenues to you while still being diligent to the physical dangers. How are parents supposed to keep their children safe now? I'll tell you it is very difficult. So while your wonder and amazement at the world has you wanting to participate, our fear has us wanting to hide you away for safekeeping because that is what we do with our most precious things.

Advice:

Listen to your intuition and hunches. Do research and utilize the process of elimination when faced with a problem. Eliminate the solutions that will not produce the desired results. It is okay for you to develop a healthy sense of adventure. Sure you will be scared, but you can show your parents that you have given serious thought into the activity. Explain your stance intelligently and thoroughly by using scenarios and possible repercussions. This may help to diminish some of the fear that they may have. Other advice I can give to gain your parents trust and reduce their anxiety, is to make solid and sound decisions about small stuff. This will build their confidence in you. Making impulsive, careless or questionable decisions will only confirm the doubts they already have. Avoid white lies. Keep your promises. Maintain any compromises that you have agreed upon such as: attending school, completing chores, and meeting curfew.

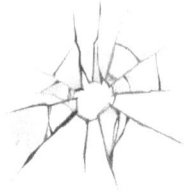

MY ILLUSION

Every spring the fair would come to town. I would usually only be able to go with my Grandma on a Sunday afternoon. Rarely would I go with my mom when she was alive. My brother was old enough to go with his friends and their families. As I got older, I'd hoped my grandma would let me go with my friends too, but no chance. Then to my surprise, I got my chance when I was 16. At that time, I spent a lot of time with my neighbors who had a daughter who was my age. She had older cousins who she was going to the fair with and they asked if I could go. After a massive amount of pleading and bargaining with my grandma, she finally agreed to let me go with them. Of course she was scared, this was my first time going at night and without adult supervision. Saturday night was when it was the most crowded, but also when it was coolest to go. So we went and I had a blast! As the night grew later, my group started to separate. Some people wanted to ride with their other friends that were there. My neighbor's boyfriend had showed up and they wanted to spend time together. While they were snuggled up on the bench kissing, I was trying to keep myself amused by the lights and the atmosphere around me. I tried telling my friend that I was getting tired and sleepy, but she didn't look like she was trying to leave anytime soon. Her cousins were lost in the crowd by now.

A couple hours later my grandma got a call from my friend saying that they couldn't find me and that they had looked everywhere for me. She told them that I was....Yep! At home in bed. Sleep! What happened was that I saw another family from our neighborhood and asked their dad if I could catch a ride home with them. He said yes and I left. You see, I knew that my grandma had nothing to fear. I knew my limits and didn't fall for peer pressure easily. I just wanted to go and not feel left out of the conversations at school on Monday. I was building her trust and confidence in me.

This didn't totally eliminate her fears because she had plenty of reservations when I left for the Navy. This would certainly stretch both of our comfort zones. I was leaving from under her protection. I would be totally reliant upon my choices and independence. In her eyes, I wasn't ready, and in a way, I wasn't. Like most teens, I wasn't prepared for adulthood. She fought against me as I tried to assert my independence. My desire to grow scared her, but she knew it was inevitable. I was determined to live on my own and experience life my way.

SHATTERING THE ILLUSIONS

Now in my 50s, a grandmother myself, and having been places she had only seen on TV, she still worried about me. That's just what parents do. During one of the last conversations we had before she died, I told her that I wanted to live on the west coast. I said to her, "don't worry about me, I've got this." She just smiled and said, "I know."

"Fear of man will prove to be a snare, but whoever trusts in the LORD is kept safe."
Proverbs 29:25

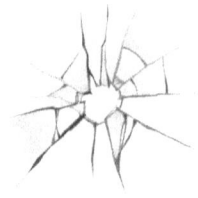

TRUTH CHECK-IN

What are some things that you can do that shows responsibility and builds others' confidence in you?

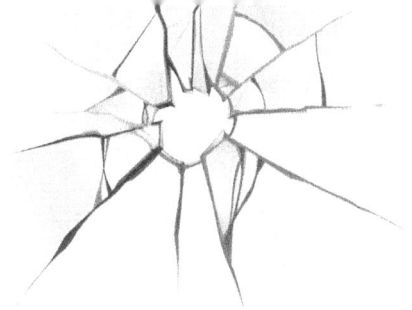

TRUTH #5
THE CHOICES YOU MAKE NOW CAN AFFECT YOU FOREVER

DO YOU EVER wonder what adults mean when they say you will pay for things in the future? You may not think that the decisions that you make now will have long term effects on your life, but they certainly can. Choices that you make as a student can affect your academic career. The choices that you make outside of school can also affect you academically and in your life in general. As a student, if you choose not to attend class or make an effort when you attend class, then you have already decided the class is not worth your time. Now you must accept any fate that comes along with that decision. Pass or fail. It was your choice and these are the results. However, what if you find out that class could help you with future endeavors? What is it worth to you now? I bet you'd wished you had made different choices. In life, for example, you choose to skip school with your friends. The day goes nothing like you planned and it wasn't nearly as fun as you thought it would be. You ended up getting in trouble that resulted in punishment. This made you miss out on a school football game that everyone but you attended. You sit and think to yourself, if I had made the choice to not skip school, none of this would have happened. Yep! That's paying for things later.

Have you seen friends or family members who seem to just have a run with bad luck? Maybe you have even experienced this yourself? Things just don't go right, there are roadblocks at every turn and you may find yourself in trouble with teachers or the authorities. Why is that? Well I can't tell you why for sure, but MY theory is that there is some type of divine intervention at work. When my plans fail or I am met with strong resistance, I use this time to stop and think. I'd ask, why is this so hard? What am I not seeing? Now I did not always do this, it took practice and some getting used to. Previously, I would try to muscle through obstacles and force my way only to still fall on my face. So I began to think maybe I am not making the best choice. What are my options? I would play out what could happen if I continue with this choice. Could my son be affected as a casualty? Utilizing those roadblocks allowed me time to think and helped me to avoid some choices that could possibly have a negative affect on future plans and endeavors.

Truth:

We don't have the foresight to know for certain how things will turn out, however, we usually have enough knowledge to predict our success rate. We see all the time in movies and on TV, the character flash back to his/her choices. It's only after the fallout or the damage has been done that they think about the alternative choices that they could have made. They are caught in a spiral of should've, could've, would've. Why couldn't they see that before? Was that alternative always an option for them? Probably so. Unfortunately sometimes we are too emotional for rational thinking. We get set on revenge or redeeming ourselves that we can't see how our actions could possibly make things worse.

Truth is, this same type of decision making can translate into your adult life. I know that the last thing that you want to consider is the future when you're trying to have fun. YOLO! You only live once..right? You probably say I have plenty of time, so right now just live for the moment. Maybe so, but sometimes that can backfire. Throwing caution in the wind could cost you a one-way ticket to the point of no return. Childhood lost, innocence lost, and opportunities lost. At best, poor choices will cause your life to be difficult.

At worst, poor choices could lead you to prison or possibly even death.

Advice:

My advice is to really give thought to your choices. Life is nothing but a series of choices and experiences. Our choices determine what our experiences will be. Sometimes other people's choices can determine or influence our experiences too. Take your time to think things through. Is it in your best interest to take this action? What are the possible outcomes? Will this affect more than just me? What kind of experience will I have? Will this have a long term effect? You have seen the stories on the news or maybe even know of friends or families who lost everything from poor choices. Some of those poor choices were made by young people. Yet some of those poor choices were made by adults. Adults who should have known better, right? They have been living a long time and should be able to make better choices. Remember, Truth #3 says adults f#% up too! We've all seen stories about the cops who choose to use excessive force when enforcing the law. However, the results seem to end in someone losing their life. At some point, they could have made a better choice. They may have needed to use excessive force initially, but once the individual was no longer a threat, was the continued use of excessive force still needed? Furthermore, as a result of the officer's choice, they are now being investigated, which could possibly end in the officer losing their job or going to prison. At the very least, some type of statement on their permanent record that will follow them for the rest of their career. Do you see how one person's decision can have multiple outcomes? Do you see how a choice that you make now can continue to affect you in the future? If the road that you are trying to travel seems difficult, take a pause and think about the results. If you need to move differently, then pivot. There is nothing wrong with switching lanes. Remember you are making sound and solid choices.

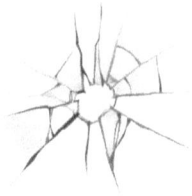

MY ILLUSION

In 1995, I was 24 years old and I was dating this guy. He was cute, funny, and a great dancer. He was only a few years older than I was, so I assumed that he had life figured out. He had a job, a car, and his own place (or so I thought). Turned out he lived with his "ex-girlfriend" and drove her car. Then he left his job shortly after we met. One night he was at my house and I had just gotten home from work. He wanted to use MY car to go hangout with his friends. He still wasn't working at the time. I told him that he could not use my car. I further said that he should be more concerned with finding a job than hanging out. He called his friend to come pick him up and began to gather his belongings to leave the house. At this point I could have chosen differently, but I stood in front of the door and tried to keep him from leaving. He pushed me down onto a glass coffee table smashing it into pieces. There was glass everywhere! My legs and arms were all cut up. I let my anger get the best of me and we began to fight, another poor choice. The police were called and he went to jail that night. About a month later, I allegedly ran a red light and was pulled over by the police. Apparently there was a warrant out for my arrest in regards to that night. I spent the night in jail and was charged with assault.

I tell you this story because even today at 50 years old, this incident still comes up during background checks. Some places may only check 10 years of your background history. The types of jobs I've had required that I disclose any criminal history regardless of length of time. Although the incident happened 25 years ago, if I don't disclose the information then that could disqualify me as a candidate. Interestingly enough, I have not been in any trouble since then. Do you think that is taken into account? Not really. I can only think of one instance where an interviewer acknowledged that that was the only blemish on my record. People will focus first on poor choices before acknowledging your accomplishments.

Do yourselves a favor and think before you make a choice. Peak into the future and give thought to those "what-if" scenarios. Understand there is no right or wrong choice. Just know you will be living with the results of whatever choice you make and be okay with it.

"...Everyone should be quick to listen, slow to speak and slow to become angry..."
James 1:19

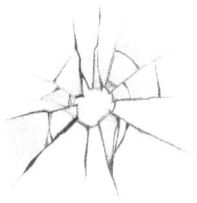

TRUTH CHECK-IN

What stood out the most to you in this chapter?
What areas can you apply this to yourself?

_____

_____

_____

_____

_____

_____

_____

_____

TRUTH #6
SEX ≠≠ LOVE; IT'S JUST SEX

THIS IS THE chapter that I will probably catch the most heat for. I like to watch the CW's *Superman and Lois* TV show. In this series, Superman is now a dad of two teenage sons. There was an episode where the boys decided to go into the family's barn, despite being instructed many times to stay out of there. During this episode they decided that this was the time to go inside. Thinking that they were old enough to handle the consequences, they go inside the barn. They ended up discovering their dad's (Superman) spaceship, however, someone got hurt in the process. They had to admit that their curiosity led to them disobeying their parents and making a poor choice. Now I bet Superman thought he was protecting his sons, but keeping them in the dark resulted in someone getting hurt. Keeping a secret went from protection to ignorance to hindrance. You are probably wondering why I am talking about Superman (LOL). It is just to show the correlation with how adults think that keeping you in the dark is protection, only to find out that their denial and lack of communication can result in harm to the very people that they are trying to protect. I certainly am not suggesting that sex should be discussed with young children. However, I think it is irresponsible of parents to blindly ignore your growing knowledge when they send you to school everyday to learn.

Truth

There are already enough misconceptions around sex in adults. I can only imagine what your perceptions are based on what you've heard. So here goes! Sex does not equal love. Those are two different things, and love means many things to many people. If you ask 10 people young or old for their definition of love, you will get 10 different descriptions for love. However, sex is just sex. Yes sex can be emotional. Actually, sex is full of emotions, and maybe one of those emotions might be love, but it might not. Not all sexual encounters mean that love is attached. Our emotions and feelings are so raw when we are young, that it is easy to project our own perceptions onto others. We can confuse kindness with flirtation. A simple compliment could be mistaken for romantic interest. So of course we can confuse sex with love. The truth is that a lot of people enter adulthood with many unanswered questions about sex. Adults think that not talking about sex will somehow make you less curious. When it could really do the opposite. It can heighten your curiosity. You have spent your whole life being told no. Remember being young and you were told NOT to do something? Just like in *Superman*, all you wanted to do was that thing or you wanted to know why you shouldn't do it. Either way, your curiosity was piqued and eventually you snuck to do it anyway. (LOL! I know you did..been there, done that). It was a poor decision on your part and you earned whatever results you received. Actually, according to the high school students surveyed in the 2019 National Youth Risk Behavior Survey conducted by Center for Disease Control, 38% of teens have had sex. The survey also reports a decrease in preventative steps being taken to prevent a STD or an unintended pregnancy. At some point parents have to equip teens with accurate facts and hope they make better choices. Open communication between both parents and teens is a great place to start.

THERE IS NO ADVICE SECTION IN THIS CHAPTER. I HAVE GIVEN YOU THE TRUTH, BUT THE FINAL CHOICE IS YOURS.

MY ILLUSION

My son was born when I was 19 years old. I had already graduated high school and was serving in the Navy. I was living on my own, but still technically a teenager. Confused and inexperienced with sex, I learned most of what I knew about sex from the guys that I dated. A few had been older, but most were my age. I thought love came with sex and vice versa. Sex was just what I was supposed to do because it was certainly expected. After all, my entire childhood I'd seen this on TV. They would say I love you to one another before, during, and after sex. I learned about sex and love through TV, friends, and magazines. I was terrified of my grandmother and I'd dare not ask my brother. Forget about it! Let's not forget my partners and who knows where they got their information from. By the time I had my son, I knew everything yet knew nothing. There was no one around who could confirm or deny my assumptions. Naturally I assumed sex equated love, especially unprotected sex. I didn't want to offend or insult my boyfriend by insisting that we use condoms. Plus, there was no need to use protection if we were in love and going to be together, right? Well five months into my pregnancy, my boyfriend (oops.. baby daddy) informed me that he didn't love me. In fact, he said that he was too young to be a father and was not ready. (Dude was like 23 or 24, but still older than me at 19). So that was that. Next I met DD who was 27. Now according to my grandmother, he was a good man because he was willing to be with me while I was pregnant with another man's child (eye roll). He stuck around for my entire pregnancy. I figured, okay then, this is what love is. Turns out he was separated from his wife and had a son of his own! WTH?! Also, I found out why his friend called him DD when I had to get treated for an STD! **SIGH**

Yes! I learned the hard way about having unprotected sex. It never occurred to me that it could happen. Like most young people, I thought I was invincible. I figured I knew all I needed to keep myself safe. I mean, I was a good judge of character and I could tell if my partner was lying, or so I thought. I remember sitting and waiting on my test results when I overheard two lab technicians discussing the "specimen sample." Talk about embarrassing. Once they realized that it was my specimen and that I could hear them, I could see they were embarrassed for me. Then one technician asked me to come inside and look into the microscope for myself. I saw a bunch of moving organisms! Of course I had looked in a microscope before during

SHATTERING THE ILLUSIONS

Biology class in high school, but what I saw then was nothing like this. He explained that the specimen was full of bacteria. Not knowing anything about my body, I asked how could it happen and he said unprotected sex with a partner who also has the bacteria. We were just passing it back and forth to each other. I was MORTIFIED! I left in tears, prescription in hand, and a realization that I knew nothing. That was a very defining moment for me and it still influences my decisions to this day. I have very honest conversations with potential partners. I talk about health, status, and suggest getting tested. No, these conversations are not sexy but are VERY necessary.

Fast forward, I am now 21 and my son is 2. I met this guy who was a suave smooth talking brother. A real chocolate dream. He said all the right things and he was in the Navy too. A military police officer. He asked me to marry him and I thought for sure this was love. I mean he put a ring on it. Well his version of love came with bumps and bruises. His idea of "foreplay" was to argue before sex. This was a complete turn off, but that didn't matter because I was his wife. Who was I gonna tell? He was the police. If he had been out drinking with the fellas after work or a softball game, I knew I wasn't getting any sleep. I was in for a long night. Have you ever been so tired, but scared to sleep? That got old really quick! One day while he was at work, I packed up my son and I never looked back. I filed for divorce in another state and that was that. I was one of the lucky ones. I know people who have endured some abusive relationships. I mean real nightmares. As time passed, I continued to confuse sex and love. I used them interchangeably. Hurting my own feelings and breaking my heart each time. I could keep blaming my partners for my choices and ignoring the red flags. It has taken many years for me to understand that sex is just sex. It is a transactional exchange of energy, emotions, and pleasure. That's it. A euphoric release that is short lived. Typically disappearing almost as rapidly as it appeared. I learned that love requires much more equity than sex does. Being in love is a different kind of nakedness and that is scary for most people. Vulnerability, compromise, and communication are complicated for some people and it's easier just to give up your body than your heart. So you settle for uncomplicated and superficial sex. However, they are missing out on the best part, and that's love and being loved.

"Are you so foolish? After beginning by means of the Spirit, are you now trying to finish by means of the flesh?"
Galatians 3:3

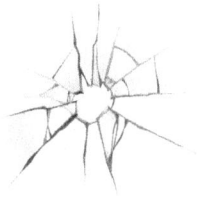

TRUTH CHECK-IN

Do you have burning questions about sex that you wish someone would just answer honestly? What are some other sex and/or love illusions that you've heard?

_____

_____

_____

_____

_____

_____

_____

_____

TRUTH #7
WE ALLOW OTHERS TO PUT LIMITS ON US

THERE ARE NO limits on you. The illusion comes in when you allow someone to put you in a box. Have you ever been told that you couldn't do something? Were you told that you're not smart enough, tall enough or slim enough? Maybe you grew up in the projects, fostercare, or a lower income household and was told that you would never amount to anything? Or did you hear something like, you're a girl; girls are supposed to be this and boys are supposed to do that. Whatever was said, is that person putting you in a box. It is not necessarily strangers, they can be the closest people to you. Parents, siblings, friends, boyfriends/girlfriends, teachers, counselors, or pastors. Any of them can offer you their opinion of what they think you are capable of, but ultimately it is up to you. They may think they are giving you solid advice, but it's up to you whether or not you accept those limits.

SHATTERING THE ILLUSIONS

I love to see the Tik Tok videos where people show their accomplishments despite being told that they couldn't or wouldn't be successful. Someone somewhere told them that they couldn't become a doctor, nurse, or whatever, and then we see them in uniform in the office or hospital. It makes me smile everytime! They refused to allow other people's opinion of them define what they are capable of doing. One story that always inspires me is from motivational speaker Lisa Nichols. Lisa talks about her experience in high school and how her English teacher told her she was a weak writer and that she should never speak in public. The teacher suggested that she get an office job and just be. Today Lisa Nichols has become one of the greatest transformational coaches. She is a sought after speaker and her conferences are always booked well in advance. She is an author and has worked with many celebrities and has appeared on TV shows like *The Oprah Winfrey Show*. Thankfully, Lisa did not accept the advice of that teacher. She is definitely one of my influencers. Her story definitely inspires me to take chances and step out of my comfort zone.

Truth:

Truth is, no one can tell you what you are capable of. So who is right, you or them? Only you can decide that. For example, you have dreams of being a lawyer and want to go to college, however your counselor tells you that you don't have the grades to get into college and you should find another career path. You really want to go to college and become a lawyer, but the counselor's advice is not aligned with your goals. So what would you do?

Sometimes the advice of others can come with good intentions, but even that kind of advice could still be stifling. It could also be wrapped in fear and jealousy. Yep jealousy! It may not sound or feel like it, but it is still jealousy. If you heard statements like, "you are better than me," or, "I could never do that," then it could be. You are attempting to do something that your family or friend would never try but you are not them. Maybe they don't have the confidence in themselves that you do. It could make you feel guilty for even trying, but do it anyway! Former president Theodore Roosevelt said, *"comparison is the thief of joy."* This means that if you spend time comparing your life to other people's lives you will miss out on your own happiness. If you are so busy thinking others are smart, brilliant, funny, and beautiful, you will not see your own smarts, brilliance, beauty, and humor. Everyone has a gift/talent to shine.

Advice:

My suggestion is that you get real serious and honest about how bad you want it. It probably hurts your feelings to hear that from your counselor, and you know that your GPA is not great, so you keep it real with yourself. If you keep applying the same effort that you always have towards school, then your counselor may be right. However, instead of the counselor suggesting to find another career path, she could have provided you with feedback on your grades and your performance. She could have explained to you that your goal requires a lot of hard work, more effort than you are putting forth, and ensuring that you understand that you need to apply yourself and be willing to do what is needed if you're really serious about being a lawyer. She could have told you that attending college requires discipline and that you need to develop strong study habits. Also how you may have to compromise your social activities. There could be many times that you will have to give up hanging out with your friends for homework.

Your counselor should confirm your understanding and that you are willing to take action toward your future. People will try to put you in a box. However, you do not have to accept it. Accepting their limitations as truth will only be true because you believe it to be. For some reason, it is other's opinion of our worth that we remember more than anything else and can influence our decisions for years to come. Moreover, even if this is your truth today, it does not have to be your truth tomorrow. Each day is a new day and another chance to be the you that you want to be. It is never too late. Begin exactly where you are.

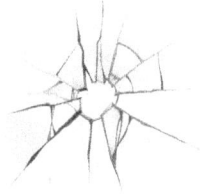

MY ILLUSION

I was 17 years old when I joined the Navy, in fact I turned 18 in boot camp. I met people of all ages and backgrounds from across the United States. I was intrigued because I found their life stories and experiences fascinating. One of my shipmates told me that she was gypsy and so was her mother and grandmother. She told me that she was a palm reader and asked if she could read my palm. "Sure," I said. I had no idea of what a gypsy was nor about palm reading. It sounded interesting so I let her read my palm. She grabbed my hand and looked at it. It was like she was spreading the skin in my hand as she tilted it back and forth. Her face was blank so I couldn't get a reaction. Finally she looked at me and said that my future read that I will never be rich. I will have financial struggles all my life. Now she said other things too, but I didn't hear anything past that. You see, I had just allowed her to put me in a box. Like most people, I had dreams of being rich and famous. Yet my acceptance of her words sealed the lid on the box. Any time that I would have financial challenges or encounter obstacles

SHATTERING THE ILLUSIONS

(like being homeless at 30), I was giving her words power. If someone had told me that I would be homeless at 30, I would have said that was NOT possible. Well that is exactly what happened, and with a 13 year old in tow. Initially I lived with a friend sharing bunk beds with her kids and my son. I slept in my car for a night or two. Then I met a young man who took me home to his mom and she graciously allowed us to live with them for a couple of months. I didn't have the support that I thought I had. I could have just stayed in that situation feeling sorry for myself and blaming everyone else, or I could have sucked it up and figured a way out. I wasn't homeless for long, but it was a very humbling 4 months.

It took years for me to realize that I gave power to someone else. I gave her words validity over my life and her words would play in my head throughout the years. I would say to myself, "well she did say for life," and continued to accept what was happening to me like I had no control over it. If the box had opened at some point, I stayed in there by my own reinforcement. Heed these words of caution. Be careful of the advice you give validity to, even the advice that comes from me. Some people mean well and are not trying to hurt you. Believe in yourself and follow your heart. Only you know your true abilities.

"We have different gifts,
according to the grace
given to
each of us."
Roman 12:6

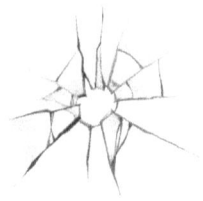

TRUTH CHECK-IN

Is there an area in your life where someone tries to put you in a box? How will you take your power back?

_____

_____

_____

_____

_____

_____

_____

_____

_____

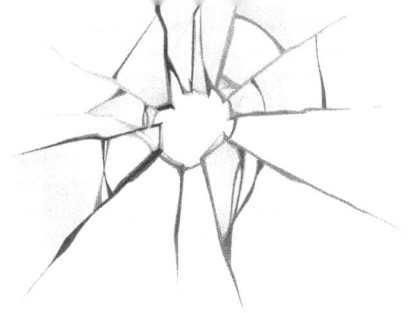

TRUTH #8
WE ALL HAVE DREAMS

EVERYONE HAS AT least once had a dream for themselves. Dreams differ from person to person and can be small or grand in size. Some people have many talents and may have dreams for each. This is the most visible in the entertainment industry. We see rappers and singers who are extremely successful in their industries and then evolve into very credible actors. They are so good as actors that you actually forget they had solid rap skills. Athletes have been successful at having crossover careers too. I guess you could say these individuals have achieved their first dream and are now following their second one. Maybe, the artist has always wanted to be an actor, but singing was the first opportunity that presented itself? Being an established singer got them an opportunity to act that they might not have gotten otherwise. I can probably guess someone somewhere along the lines advised them against switching to another career because, why mess up a good thing? Thank goodness the artist didn't listen, had a vision for themselves and confidence in their abilities. We would have missed out on some great acting performances. I'm sure the person who offered the advice thought that they were suggesting what was best for them. However, they were not giving any consideration to who the artist is and what accomplishments they saw for themselves.

In the span of your lifetime, you will have many dreams. You will have a dream career, dream life or dream vacation. They are all something to work toward. Some are interconnected and reliant upon achieving the other first. Maybe initially income and lifestyle is the fuel to chase the career, but once you achieve success then what? As you accomplish one dream you become more confident in your abilities to reach the others so you begin to challenge yourself and dream bigger. Maybe there is something else that you are talented at doing? Think about those artists who actually took the advice and decided not to pursue their other dreams. Do you think they might have regrets? Is it possible they would have been successful at that too? We have seen entertainers who were able to pivot become successful businessmen and women. Some are more successful at business than they were in entertainment. We see them begin to give back to their communities and hometowns. They start foundations and create scholarships to sponsor another's dream.

Truth:

Truth is, chasing your dreams is hard..but what in life isn't? The way I see it, regular and everyday living is hard too so you might as well spend some time chasing your dreams too. We all encounter dream killers who will caution against every move you make and give you all the reasons in the world not to try. The problem is that they never offer any other solutions or alternatives with their objections. They may also provide poorly supported or no examples at all. Let's examine this a bit further. Take the statement, "I tried that before and it did not work for me." Now you may think that that is some quality advice and giving you the heads up. But are they only sharing their results without sharing any specific details?

Details such as:

1. When did they try and was there a market for it? Timing can play a factor, especially if you are trying to introduce something new.
2. How long did they try? It may take multiple attempts before success is achieved. Rarely is success obtained at first attempt or overnight.
3. What actions did they take and how are they similar to yours? No doubt you could experience some similar challenges and the steps they took to overcome them.

SHATTERING THE ILLUSIONS

4. What do they wish they'd known? It is okay to give serious consideration to advice from someone who is detailed and transparent.

Pursuing your dreams is totally about you and the amount of effort that you're willing to put towards it. While initially you might only be chasing your dream on a part-time basis, there will come a time when it will require you to fully commit to it. This means that sacrifices will be required. Have you heard the term "starving artist?" They are called that because of the sacrifices they make for their dream. They may work and make just enough money to pay rent and bills. They may only eat one meal a day or very small meals like ramen noodles or PB&J sandwiches. Some deal with bouts of homelessness too. This was their level of commitment. However, if this is not the level of commitment that you are wanting to give then that is okay. Just be ready for what sacrifice means for you.

I have met people who have lived their lives exactly how society told them to. They got a good job, got married, and raised their kids. They should be happy right? However, they would say to me that they can't help but feel like something is missing and that there has to be more to life. My guess is that they stopped dreaming. Some people think dreaming is a young person's game but it is not. Dreams are for dreamers! Just because you grow older doesn't mean you stop dreaming. Our dreams evolve as we do. Aspects that appealed to us at 20 years old may not appeal to us when we are 35, but there is still a variation of that dream within us. We have to review and possibly redefine what achieving that dream means at 35, 40, or 50 years old.

Advice:

My advice is to not allow anyone or anything to kill your dreams. However, don't be out there unprepared either. Do your research. Know what is required of you and decide if you are willing to make the sacrifices needed at this time. Don't be fooled by that overnight success stuff you see in the movies. It is a lot of hard work! If you talk to people in the career you're interested in, they will tell you about the hard work they put in or are still putting in. Your success depends on your conviction and dedication to your dream. Just because it didn't work for others does not mean it won't work for you. You are not them. They can provide good experiences that you can learn from, but your success or failures are based on your commitment. The most important advice that I can offer is to remember that you live in the real world. There will still be real adult issues that you encounter while you're chasing your dreams. The lucky people have a support system that will allow them the freedom to pursue their dreams. However, some people have to provide for themselves and chase the dream at the same time. You might have to chase your dreams and work a regular job at the same time. It could require you to dedicate time before and/or after your regular job and most likely on your days off. Consider the tools you need and how you will pay for them. Do you need studio time? A producer? Easels and paint? Models? Fabric? Makeup? A stylist chair and accessories? Do you see where I am going with this? You will each have different needs but everyone's needs will be concerned with cost and paying for them. During my time as a career advisor, students would share with me that they felt like they had to choose between getting a job and chasing their dream. They felt that by choosing to learn a trade, they were giving up on their dream. I would advise them that they did not have to give up on their dream. I told them it did require them to assess their level of commitment to their dream and if it was something they were willing to make sacrifices for at this time. I'd say that it will be hard but if they are ready to do the work, then they could still move towards that dream. If they were not ready for that level of commitment or simply not able to put in the work at that time, then to pause their endeavors towards the dream for a little while and focus on the immediate need.

 This doesn't mean give up, but allow the dream to breathe. Sometimes, timing is everything! Time restraints can be another dream killer. I am not talking about deadlines. Those are different. Deadlines are great because it keeps you accountable and working to complete the small goals that you have set for yourself. Small accomplishments, or as the transformational coach Lisa Nichols calls it, "needlepoint movements," keep the momentum going. No, time restraints are putting unnecessary pressure on yourself to complete some impossible goal that you have set for yourself. Time restraints are stressful and draining. They rarely make you feel empowered. It is actually just the opposite, they can inflate a failure and make it feel worse than it really is. An example of this is stating, "if I have not completed this thing by age 25 or 30, then it's never gonna happen for me." DO NOT do that to yourself. As I said earlier, timing is everything.

Here's the thing, dreams never expire. Some will tell you that you're too old to dream or that you should give up on a certain dream, but if it's YOUR dream then only you can put a limit on it. This is what I know, sometimes you can achieve your dream without even trying. You can also achieve one dream while chasing another. Dreams take hard work and can take a long time to manifest. Sometimes you have to take a break and relax. While on break, inspiration hits and you get ideas on what actions to take towards the dream. Or perhaps you meet someone who has a connection or information on the resources you would need. Then just like that, you have made it to the next level of your dream! It can happen just that fast and out of nowhere. All you did was take a step back, look at the big picture, and allow creativity to flow in.

Another dream killer is comparison. Like time restraints, comparing yourself to others in the industry or in your age range will again inflate any fears or failures that you experience. Especially in the information age of social media where everybody seems to have the perfect everything, comparison must not be given life at all. Instead, run your race. Do what makes you feel strong, confident, and intelligent. The only person that you are competing against is you. Be your brilliant, talented, awkward, complex, nerdy but cool and fancy self. There is no comparison. NO ONE CAN BE YOU BETTER THAN YOU.

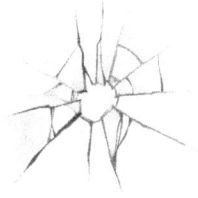

MY ILLUSION

I always thought that I had to have life, career, and family figured out by a certain age. The age I had determined for myself was age 30. Well that didn't actually happen, just the opposite! Instead at that age, I found myself homeless and completely changing my life! That's another story for another time so for now I'll tell you a different one. Society made me feel like I was supposed to have everything figured out in my 20s. I thought that I should have a plan for the move I was to make and act accordingly. It seems that I was not as accomplished as the other 30 year olds that I knew. Even some of my younger friends appeared more put together than I was. So when things didn't go as planned, I felt stressed and like I was behind. I then put my foot on the imaginary gas and was in a hurry to catch up. I had not yet figured out "what I wanted to be when I grew up." I didn't have a college degree and I was working odd and end jobs. At one time, I had many dreams and I felt that I could do a lot of things. However if you remember in Truth #7, I allowed myself to be put in a box. Let me pause to say that, no one around me told me that I was behind or late to the party. This was all MY perception of my reality. So as I grew older, my dreams fell farther away. They turned into little fantasies that I used to escape reality when I needed a brain break. By now, I had decided to go to college. So I was in school, working two jobs, picking up shifts here and there as a banquet server during special events, and raising my son. Yeah when I applied pressure to myself, I APPLIED PRESSURE! Ironically, I still felt this was not enough. (This is not a good trait. Over the years I have worked on being nicer to myself.) Anyway by the time I was 40, my son had graduated high school, joined the military, and began adulting for himself. I found myself unhappy with everything about me. I thought, what happened to me? When did I stop dreaming? I had so many things I wanted to do and places to see. (That damn box!) One day I was listening to *The Steve Harvey Morning Show* on the radio and there was a guy who called into the show to speak to Steve. The caller began to tell Steve a story about how he was 40 years old and he thought that it was too late in life for him to start over and chase his dream. He felt that he had wasted so much time and now he was too old. Steve said that he understood how the caller felt but told him this was not the time to give up. Steve went on to ask the caller, "what if you live another 40 years and still had not tried to achieve your dream?" He asked the caller if he was still able to chase his dream? The caller said yes and that he had just been lost and felt hope was gone. Steve said to him, "if you feel like you have wasted 40 years of life, then make the next 40 count. What you don't want to do is be 80 years old and have done nothing." That show was almost 10 years ago and I still remember those words. Hearing the advice Steve gave to that caller lit a fire in me as well. I was inspired to find a new life for myself and I am determined to make these next 40 count! I am forever grateful that I was able to hear that show. Thanks Steve!

My belief is that we stop living when we stop dreaming. I had a friend from Africa who was 90 years old, we called her Grandma Sarah. I enjoyed spending time with her, listening to her stories about growing up in Tanzania. We would talk about her experiences as a woman in her country and her activism efforts. Now a small, shy, soft-spoken woman, she told me there was a time in her life that people would have pried the microphone from her hands during protests. She was still very active in her church, fundraising and working with local nonprofits. The most inspiring thing about Grandma Sarah was her determination to earn her citizenship. She studied tirelessly for the exam. The morning of her examination, we sat in a restaurant and had breakfast. She handed me her study guide and asked me to quiz her. As I bounced around the study guide asking her questions, I was amazed that she got them all correct. She would pause to think for a minute and then give me the answer in detail. She was nervous but determined to see it through as we left the restaurant. The big smile on her face as she walked back to the car told me everything. She passed her naturalization test and at 91 year old she achieved her dream of becoming a U. S. citizen. As the group of about 60 people of all ages, races and cultures took their oath of citizenship, I sat watching the proud faces of accomplishment. It was a profound thing to see. They had each taken different paths to manifest the same dream they shared that afternoon. At the start of 2020, Grandma Sarah was preparing to return to her country to see her family and visit the town where she grew up. The last time I saw her, she asked if I would help her upon her return. You see she had already begun working on her next dream of writing a book. She was writing about how fortunate she was to witness president Barack Obama be sworn into office. She never thought that she would see a Black U.S. president in her lifetime. We lost contact due to the quarantine, so I don't know if she ever made it home. I want to tell Grandma Sarah that I am forever grateful for your friendship. Thank you for showing me that as long as I am alive, I will always have a dream in my spirit.

Today at 50 years old, I am still chasing dreams! You might hear them called bucket lists but it is one in the same. There are still many things that I want to experience and places that I want to visit and live. I am just now learning to stop putting time restraints on myself and to stop thinking that I am behind. Behind what and according to who? We all have different journeys and the experiences are not the same. Some people may journey with you and some may not. You will make new friends and old friends may leave to have experiences of their own. That's normal. As you change, your life will change too. Memories are made in the experiences. I have learned that the beauty, the fun, and even the pain, are all in the journey, not in the destination. Chasing my dreams is where I learned the most about myself. Like how resilient and resourceful I am. I bet that you are too. Avoid that box! You will surprise yourself.

"You will be betrayed even by parents, brothers and sisters, relatives and friends, and they will put some of you to death."
(Luke 21:16)

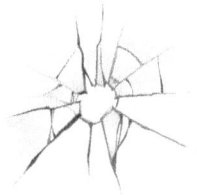

TRUTH CHECK-IN

Dreams are born in a creative space. Use the space below to write, draw, color, or whatever feels authentic, to create your dream.

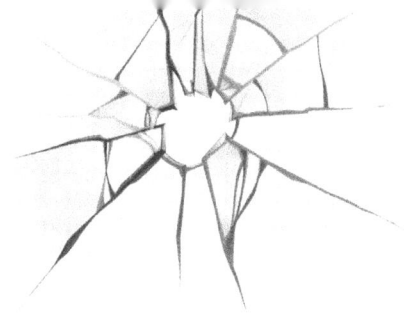

TRUTH #9
FINANCIAL LITERACY

LET'S TALK ABOUT being financially responsible. What is debt? Merriam-Webster Online Dictionary defines debt as, "a state of being under obligation to pay or repay someone or something in return for something received." Now there are different types of debt such as owing a friend a favor. However, in this chapter, I want to talk about financial debt. I'm not sure why adults do not talk about finances with teens. I assume that possibly it is because back when we were in school, there were classes like Home Economics. In Home Ec., we gained basic knowledge, or what we know today as Life Skills. We were taught skills like cooking, sewing, and home repairs, and budgeting skills like balancing a checkbook. Furthermore, with advances in banking like debit cards, auto-pay, and online checking accounts, the need to write checks has almost become obsolete. Yes these things make life easier, but in my opinion it also makes it easier to get into debt.

According to Experian.com, "a short-term personal loan is designed to be repaid within a year, or even just a couple weeks depending on the loan." In my opinion, short term loans are the easiest to get but are also the easiest to get you into financial trouble. Some types of short term loans are:

Payday Loan: Loan that you make against your paycheck. This loan tends to be smaller in amount, therefore is paid back in a lump payment (with interest). These loans are due on your next pay cycle. They are set up and you are required to provide access to your bank account. This loan is automatic so money will be taken from your account automatically. So be sure the money is in the account.

Title Loan: Loan that you can make against the title of your car. Your car is the collateral for the loan ensuring that you pay it back. The loan amount will vary based on your need and the year and condition of the car. The terms for buying back title to your car (the loan) will be set based on the amount loaned. Failure to pay this loan back will result in losing your car for good.

Pawn Loan: Similar to a title loan, this type of loan also requires a personal item to use as collateral for the loan. The collateral for this type of loan can vary: jewelry, TVs, video games and gaming systems, etc. These too are short term loans, however, some lenders will allow you to make payments (instead of a lump sum) towards buying back your items. Failure to make payments will result in you losing your items. Then you might have a chance to buy them at the ticket price decided by the store owner.

Some items, especially jewelry, could be just sold in bulk to another business and you will never see your items again.

Personal Loan: Usually no collateral is required to obtain this loan, however the lender will access your credit history. Your income and credit history will be the determining factors on the amount of money that can be loaned to you. The terms and payment amount is also determined by the lender. Failure to make payments can result in negative entries on your credit report, which can affect your ability to make future purchases using credit, like buying a car or moving into an apartment.

If you decide to use any of these services, please understand the terms and interest rate of your loan.

Truth (Part 1):
The truth is, lacking financial responsibility can make it easier to incur debt. You could also spend a lifetime trying to pay it off. For young adults, it could seem so easy to qualify for credit. Credit cards, car loans, department store credit cards, or lines of credit for furniture and electronics. I remember that I thought having a checking account and a credit card was like having free money. Man was I sadly mistaken! You MUST have money in the checking account to cover your purchase before swiping your debit card, or in my case, writing the check. Some banks will allow a charge to the account to be paid, but then charge you an

overdraft fee if there is not enough money to cover it. So you could end up paying an amount up to $50 for a $20 purchase. Then there is the non-sufficient fund (NSF) fee. This fee can be charged to you by the bank if they reject a charge because there was not enough money in the account when it was posted. An example of this is: Your checking account has $40. Your lunch (with tip) costs $20. Then you buy a shirt that is $20 plus tax. Both charges are paid at the time but later the bank rejects the lunch because when the restaurant submitted the final total there was not enough money in the account. The shirt was $20 plus tax so the taxes were paid from a portion of the money that you used for lunch. Depending on how they are set up, some businesses can take the money from your checking account right away and others may take a day or two. You would need to make a deposit to add more money to cover your purchases. It is easy to miscalculate the transactions in your checking account. Now with a credit card (including department store cards), you are issued a card with a specified spending amount which could range initially from $200 to $500+. Using this card is your promise to pay the creditor later for purchases that you make now. You could pay off the full purchase amount or make payments on the balance. Either is acceptable for the creditor, however, you MUST at least make the minimum payment amount owed. These types of credit cards send monthly reports to the credit bureaus on your repayment abilities. So failing to make the minimum payment could reflect negatively on your credit report. In the future, this will affect your buying power to make big purchases like smart phones, computers, or car loans. Here again we are talking about making smart choices. I know you are probably saying that you are too young to worry about a credit score but trust me you are not. Your credit score influences the buying power you have with banks and lenders. It proves to them your ability to keep your promises to pay the money owed. The better score you have the stronger your buying power and you can even get more favorable percentage rates. A strong score can affect the amount of down payment needed to purchase a smart phone or car.

Advice (Part 1):

Educate yourself as much as possible before making any financial commitments. Research interest rates and annual percentages. Ask about reward programs and cash back options. Being knowledgeable before you make purchases might balance your emotions when buying. We tend to become emotionally attached to an item when making decisions. We really want that car, those sneakers, or those earrings, and this could lead to us making emotional purchases. We have fantasized about how we would look in the car or wearing the earrings or sneakers, and some are willing to make it happen regardless of the cost. Emotional decisions like this and a lack of financial literacy could push you to make impulsive purchases. Please take the time to understand your finances. Learn how to create a budget. Open a savings account, most banks will offer one when you open a checking account. Read through contracts before you sign anything and ASK QUESTIONS! Your financial future depends on it.

This truth briefly discusses a couple of areas surrounding money. However, a good book for you to read is *Real Money Answers - College Life & Beyond* by Patrice C. Washington. Patrice is a personal finance coach and in this book she dives into the beliefs and myths around money. She talks about your money mindset and the way it affects how you view money and your relationship with it. Patrice also shares techniques and life hacks to teach you how to manage money and develop a healthy relationship with money. She truly is a money maven and I am sure her book would be a valuable resource for you.

Truth (Part 2):

Next is paying for college. Students who are college bound or planning to enroll in a training program after school have the concern of paying for their education. Some are fortunate enough to secure funding through scholarships. Others have parents who are able to pay for their education.

Then there are those students whose option for funding relies mostly on financial aid or student loans.

Advice (Part 2):

My advice? Apply for every scholarship that you are eligible for. Even if your parents are planning to pay for your education, you should still apply. There are specific requirements to determine eligibility or maintain your eligibility, so be sure that you read and follow the instructions completely. Get assistance from parents, teachers, and counselors if needed. Then there is financial aid. Again, even if your parents plan to pay, you still should apply for financial aid. You want to take advantage of whatever opportunities are available to you. Your parents will appreciate any help they receive. There are different types of financial aid opportunities such as federal and state assistance. For instance in Georgia, they have the HOPE grant/scholarship available for their residents. When I attended college in Georgia, I was eligible for the Federal Pell Grant and the HOPE grant. Also some colleges or programs offer scholarships as incentive for enrollment. As a student at Arizona State University, I was able to take advantage of small scholarships that were offered. However, some of my classmates had full scholarships because they were planning on becoming a teacher or simply because they worked for Starbucks. It would be best for you to make an appointment and speak with a Financial Aid Advisor at the college to find out the opportunities that you are eligible for.

Financial Aid Advisors are a resource provided to you by the college so why not use them? They are up-to-date on policy and procedures for attending college. They have access to a wealth of information on obtaining grants and scholarships for school. They can help you apply for tuition assistance if that is offered through your current job. There are some advisors that specialize in assisting veterans with attending college using their G.I. Bill. Whatever your need may be, it is worth a trip to the Financial Aid Office.

Finally there are student loans. At one point during my academic career, I had to use student loans to pay for college. I will say that I am thankful that I had that option, but I admit I did make some poor choices concerning them. Unlike scholarships and grants that don't have to be paid back, you are 100% obligated to pay student loans back. Hence the keyword "Loan." If you must get a student loan, do your due diligence and make sure that you understand the mechanics surrounding student loans. Find out the type of loan it is, does it accrue interest, who is the lender and when are the payments due? These are some of the things that I neglected to find out about. Another hack for student loans is to only accept the amount you need to cover the cost for classes and books. Your loan offer could be more than your expenses and that "extra money" may seem nice but remember you still have to pay everything back. Once you agree to the terms and accept it, then it is yours.

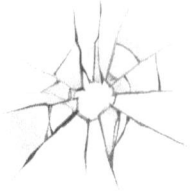

MY ILLUSION

Money management skills is something that you will hopefully develop throughout your adulthood. Initially I thought it wasn't that hard. I watched my grandmother pay bills all the time. She worked, we always had food and occasionally ate out at restaurants. So I figured budgeting was easy. The summer of my senior year of high school I learned a valuable lesson. Senior year is the pinnacle of my ending for childhood. We commemorate the accomplishment with senior pictures, class rings, yearbooks, cap and gown, invitations, and trading cards. Don't forget about prom, the senior trip, and other senior activities. Well I wanted it all! I wanted to experience everything senior year had to offer. I was also a member of my school's choir. We traveled and performed throughout the state as well as all over the U.S. Our choir attire had to stay performance ready at all times. (Shout out to all the Jones High Sugarlumps!!) As you probably guessed, my grandmother was not as excited about my senior year as I was. In addition to real life bills, *this* was a big financial obligation. She had to be honest with me and let me know that she could not afford all the things that I wanted. I had to pick one, maybe two things and that was it. She said that if I wanted all the other things that I would have to pay for it myself. It's not that she was trying to teach me a lesson or didn't want me to have those things, she simply could not afford them. We had never discussed budgeting or money management, and at 16 years old, I simply did not understand. So in the summer of 1988, I got my first job as a cashier. My grandmother had taken me to open a savings account with her credit union. I did not know about checking accounts and I don't think she did either. I had only seen her pay bills with cash or money orders. I saved my paychecks and I was able to pay for the majority of my senior activities on my own. My grandmother bought my prom dress as a reward for all my hard work. I was proud of myself and felt a sense of accomplishment, however, there was much about financial literacy that I didn't know. Later, I wished that I had known about loans, credit cards, and money management. I thought that the lack of money was the reason for my problems and that having it would solve them. Boy was I wrong. I would spend most of my adult life chasing money. It seemed that despite the more money I made, it was still somehow never enough. I finally learned and understood how my mindset and how I felt about money affected my relationship with money. This is why

SHATTERING THE ILLUSIONS

I share my truth with you. Develop a healthy relationship with money. Know your limits and set boundaries for yourself. You determine your worth! No one can do that for you and you shouldn't let them either.

"Whoever loves money never has enough; whoever loves wealth is never satisfied with their income...."
(Ecclesiastes 5:10)

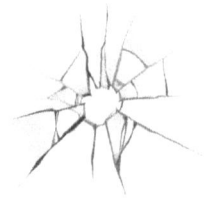

TRUTH CHECK-IN

What questions do you have about money, banking, student loans, and financial aid? Remember: All questions are important when planning your financial future.

_____

_____

_____

_____

_____

_____

_____

_____

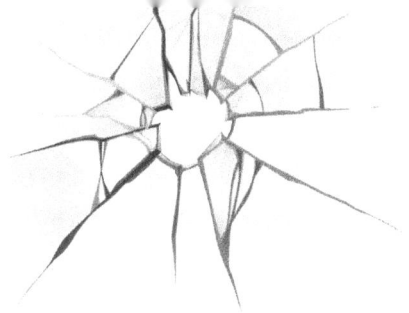

TRUTH #10
LIVE IN THE MOMENT

HAVE YOU HEARD the saying, "stop and smell the flowers?" What do you think that means? Literally, it means that when you see flowers, you can enjoy not only their beauty but also their fragrance. Metaphorically however, this means to live in the moment. Enjoy your surroundings, your partner, friends, and family. Create memories and experiences. I like to go on road trips. I enjoy driving and seeing the different landscapes as I drive throughout the country. There are people who don't like to drive or ride long distances. They just want to get to the destination. Some of my friends are like that too. When asked why I like to drive, I explain that I find it relaxing and it gives me time to think. I like to discover the hidden gems within the state along the way. If I am not rushed, I like to pull over and take pictures or walk a nature trail. Maybe stop for lunch at a local restaurant that I've seen on TV. Sure I am just as excited to get to the destination as well. Yet, I also know the value of the memories (good or bad) that

SHATTERING THE ILLUSIONS

are created along the way. For generations, people were taught that they were supposed to work hard all their lives and when they retire, THEN they can begin to smell the flowers and create memories. Growing up I was told to go to school, get a good job, keep my head down, and work hard to achieve the American dream. But I always thought, my dream is not the same as yours. There are many opinions on what living your life means. America was once called the land of opportunity and many people would come to America to live their life. America is composed of many cultures and their experiences. It is a great opportunity to appreciate our differences, to discover new cultures, and most times, in your very own city.

Enjoy your surroundings, your friends and experiences. Do you have that one friend who is always on social media taking and posting selfies or texting? Don't they always seem to miss THE moment? They miss the winning shot or dunk at the basketball game, the cute guy or hot girl that just passed by. The first thing they say is, "what did I miss?" That's not living in the moment! Participate and be present instead of missing out on all the fun. Nothing is worse than sharing stories and someone asks for your input and you can't contribute. Your friends actually want to hear your story, but you missed it because you were distracted. Give yourself permission to disconnect from online for a while and tap into life in real time.

Truth:

My intent was the same as other young mothers, which was to give my child the life I never had. I wanted him to travel and have experiences. You know, live in the moment. I wanted to expose him to as much life that I was able to. There was a whole world outside of what he knew. There are beautiful women all over the world. He had plenty of time for dating and sex and there was no rush for either. I didn't want him to have limited thinking the way that I did when I was his age.

The unfortunate part is that America's overt racism towards Black people makes it very difficult to live in the moment. We want the same experiences as anyone else. We like to try different foods and restaurants. We want to travel and fly first class and stay in nice hotels. We like to camp and go RVing across the country, stopping at the cool landmarks and learning about the city and town. The problem is that somehow America has the idea that we don't like these things, can't afford these things, or can't appreciate culture. I wonder where they could have gotten that idea. It is these experiences that make life interesting and worth living! If you say that Black people choose to accept the illusion of oppression, then America chooses to accept the illusion that Black people are lazy and can't appreciate fine things. Both are subjective concepts so neither should be considered as 100% truth. Not all Black

SHATTERING THE ILLUSIONS

people come from meager beginnings. Those that do are not all criminals either. Families who fall in the low income range still pay taxes, obey the law, and like nice things. Yet still those stereotypes about Black people have been perpetuated for generations. Even other cultures, who we have no beef with, have accepted this illusion about Black people. Let's be real, there are lazy people and criminals in all cultures of all races. Black people hold no patent to that. It amazes me when I hear statements like, "go back to your country." We are all immigrants here. Are we not called the melting pot? There is only one group of people who are native to the land and can truly lay claim to that statement, so how is that conveniently forgotten? Forgotten or intentionally ignored? America wants to keep a knee on our necks (metaphorically and literally)! This is the land of opportunity, the land where dreams are made, and the Declaration of Independence says that we have the right to "Life, Liberty and the pursuit of Happiness." In my opinion that statement is a written representation of living in the moment. Wikipedia states, "The phrase gives three examples of the unalienable rights which the Declaration says have been given to all humans by their creator, and which the governments are created to protect." Yet it seems like if Black people are too free or successful outside of the "acceptable" careers, we are persecuted for trying to live according to that statement. As if we offended someone for even daring to live and dream. America has villainized our sons and objectified our daughters. They are barely past puberty and being "mistaken" for 20 year olds. So the phrase takes on a whole new meaning. When we say "live in the moment," we mean just that, LIVE. In 2021, parents of Black teens and young adults still caution their loved ones to do whatever is necessary for them to live if they find themselves in intense situations, much like their enslaved ancestors. This is not to insinuate that these young people create the intense situation, however, we have seen how seemingly normal situations can escalate in the blink of an eye. What is acceptable and non-threatening behavior for others becomes aggressive and life threatening for Blacks. Being a teenager means to have a chance to learn from stupid mistakes and poor decisions. Children should be able to be children in their homes, in their schools and in their neighborhoods. It saddens me when I hear that someone has lost their life over simple altercations that escalated to a fatality for no good reason. Where fear, lack of training, and poor decision making (both from authorities and civilians) have resulted in multiple families losing a loved one. When leaving our homes for the day, everyone has the same goal and that is to return home that night. As we are walking out the door and turn to look at the task we left behind and say, I will do it when I return. Noone assumes that they will not make it home.

SHATTERING THE ILLUSIONS

In my opinion, there is fear AND jealousy toward Black people. Fear because there is an obvious effort to deny, discredit, and discourage Black Amercians. Jealousy because despite these efforts, we are still succeeding. We are a resilient group of people. I attended Steve Harvey's Act Like A Success business conference where Todd Chrisley, from the TV show *Chrisley Knows Best*, was the guest speaker. Mr. Chrisley explained his way to identify when someone is jealous of you. He stated that people only hate those who they have determined are doing better than them. My interpretation of that speech is this: Rarely will you see someone hating on another who is doing worse than them because why would they? If someone is worse off than you are then you would not envy their situation or circumstances. However, if you perceive that their situation or circumstance is better than yours then you may feel slighted. I say that White Americans feel that no one (specifically Black Americans) should get any type of "advantage" **before** they do. It is okay if it is an opportunity that they themselves have turned down or felt was beneath them. Similar to the food, clothes, and other hand me downs that plantation owners gave to the slaves. As I stated before, we are a resilient and resourceful group of people. We take scraps and junk and create masterpieces. We will find the miracle and the beauty of a thing. We will find use out of things deemed useless by others. What is meant to be an insult to us, we find a reason to be grateful for instead. Have you played a video game against the computer and you kept losing? No matter how hard or smart you play, you just can't win. So what do most people do? They press the reset button and restart the game to stop the computer's winning streak. That is my analogy for America towards Black people. They can't stand to see Black people winning so they change the rules and reset the game.

Advice:

Have adventures and enjoy your experiences starting right now. Why should you have to wait until a certain time before you can do that? There is no need to wait until old age before you can enjoy life. Some may view waiting as a reward for working hard all their lives, but why not reward yourself as you go? Rewarding yourself and celebrating milestones or accomplishments along the way can serve as motivation to keep going. So my advice is to live in the moment. Create memories and find adventures in everyday life. Serving in the military allowed me to make friends and meet people from around the world. I lived in several states and traveled to other countries. I remember thinking how fortunate I was to have that experience as a young woman. Before that, I had only been around my neighborhood. I lived in Florida so there were many places to visit, however, I had hardly gone to any. Can you imagine living less than one hour from the beach and never going? Living in the moment is to find wonder in your surroundings. Most towns have their own uniqueness. From shops, local cafes, and coffee houses, there is much to see and do. Many events like cultural festivals and carnivals take place over the weekend and are free to attend. This is an excellent opportunity to learn about others in your community. What a great way to show support and respect for their culture. Consider taking a journey to other cities within the state. You could discover new hobbies and interests like camping and hiking, or seasonal activities like kite or hot air balloon festivals. There is no one way on HOW to live in the moment, just do what makes you feel free.

Some adults don't learn to live in the moment until later in life. On your journey through adulthood, you will begin to hear people talk about purpose. Or begin wondering about why they were born. They think, "there has to be more to life." Maybe what they are really wondering is what good have I given the world? This can happen at any age, but most often with adults who have grown children. Once the kids are all independent and living on their own, they are lost. For some, this is the time that they can appreciate living in the moment. For others, this will take time because they've lost their identity. An example is a woman whose whole life had been being a mother. Raised her kids, attended PTA meetings, organized school events and fundraisers, chaperoned field trips, and carpooled for practices and games. She's a mom and enjoys being one. As the kids grow, her school involvement may lessen but that is okay because she still runs the house. Then the kids graduate and decide that they want to leave home. So what happens to the woman? The purpose she has identified with for the last 20 years has now changed drastically. She is still a mom, but now she has to redefine what her purpose is in this life. This is what I mean by losing her identity. Her whole life has been about her family and now she gets to make it about herself, but that is easier said than done. She will have to recognize the illusions in her life. The limits she has accepted from others, the fears she has in her abilities, remember the dreams she once had and develop the courage to chase them again. That's a lot of work, and some adults think that it is too hard to do at their age.

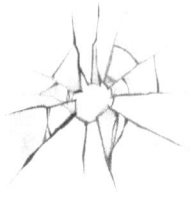

MY ILLUSION

Again, I did not always make the best decisions. I was trying to figure out life and who I was while at the same time trying to raise a son. His father was not around. His father was in the military as well and we had plans to marry and raise our family. I got reassigned to another duty station and he had been discharged and was supposed to join me. About two weeks passed and he still hadn't arrived and the phone calls had stopped altogether. Then one day I received a letter in the mail from him. He told me in the letter that he wasn't ready to be a father and I never heard from him again. As time passed, I was lucky to find a community of friends who were more like family. My son had step parents who played integral parts at different times in his life. I am grateful for them both. I can't express enough gratitude to my community family and the lessons that I learned from them.

Identity crisis showed up for me in December 2014 when my grandmother died. I was single so I was not a wife, girlfriend, or bae to anyone. I was still a mom but my son was on his own and living far away from home. My grandchildren were very young so their mom was their whole world. I was just working a regular 9 to 5 job to pay the bills and had no real responsibility. My grandmother and I had gotten really close in her later years. We talked almost everyday and I visited her more often than I ever had before. She had me and I had her. It was as if we were all we had. When she died I was lost. The title of granddaughter that I held so tightly, was now gone. For the second time in my life, I felt abandoned. First when my mom died, and now I found myself alone again. The one person who l was CERTAIN that loved me and proud of me was gone. My purpose was gone! I spent 2015 grieving and feeling depressed and lonely. I didn't want anyone to know that I was suffering so I would force on a smile. I thought, why am I here? Who would notice if I disappeared? Would anyone come looking for me? It was a very dark time for me. So, what happened, you wonder?

Well what had happened was this. I was taking night classes at the time and I didn't feel fully supported by the school. Listening to *The Steve Harvey Morning Show*, I learned there was a seminar being held by money maven Patrice Washington. I convinced a few coworkers to attend the seminar with me. Patrice was very resourceful and inspiring, but what stood out to me was her personal story about how she overcame adversity in her life. She spoke about how volunteering her time with a local nonprofit set her on her new life course. The rest of that weekend, I thought about her story and how I could apply that to my life. Since I was so frustrated with my school, I decided that I too would volunteer to gain experience and become more marketable in the workforce. I applied to volunteer with Goodwill of North Georgia, and thanks to exec April Smith, who championed on my behalf for the chance. She saw my potential despite the fact that I had a misdemeanor assault charge in my background. Remember I said back in Truth #5 that our choices can affect us forever? I was not going to mess this opportunity up. Thanks April! I began teaching classes with Goodwill's Workforce Training Program and I loved it! I was working with different people from all walks of life and at different stages in their careers. I met people who wanted to hear what I had to say. Who knows they might find something helpful. I realized my path as a career advisor. Just like that, no more identity crisis. I found my purpose! It was then that I decided to stop feeling sorry for myself, live in the moment, and focus on something bigger than me.

What I know about purpose is this, everyone has the same purpose. That purpose is to help other people. Now the area and type of help we give will differ because we all have different talents and experiences to pull from. However, we all want to accomplish the same thing and that is to spare someone else from having to endure the trouble and pain that we have. We want to give to others the thing, service, or advice that we wished we had. In my case, this book is the advice that I wished I'd had. Another thing that I thought, was that my purpose only included, supported, and benefited my family. However, just as there have been people from my past whose words and presence in my life inspired me to take action (some don't even know it), I am here to support others too. You will encounter people that you may never see again but they come to you right when you need it. There were teachers, college professors, supervisors, coworkers, and friends who I learned from. I observed them and determined how I wanted and did not want to show up in life. Understand that others may be influenced by your actions.

It was this experience where I learned to live in the moment. How depressed was I to be thinking there was nothing left for me here. I had worried my whole life about other people's acceptance of me that I never saw my own value. I couldn't appreciate the beauty and love that I had around me. While I care for and love my own family, my existence includes my service to others. I intend to spend the remainder of my life living in the moment. Appreciating the people and experiences as they come. I encourage you to live in your moments and leave no stone unturned.

"Don't let anyone look down on you because you are young, but set an example for the believers in speech, in conduct, in love, in faith and in purity."
(1 Timothy 4:12)

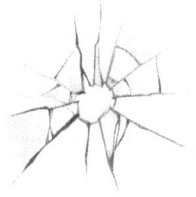

TRUTH CHECK-IN

What difficult experiences have you had so far?
Did they affect you or anyone you know? How?

_____

_____

_____

_____

What types of experiences do you want to have? How
will you live in the moment on your next adventure?

_____

_____

_____

_____

SHATTERING THE ILLUSIONS

This concludes the 10 truths about adulthood that you should know. I pray that my personal truths and advice were useful and easy to apply. My hope is that you will refer back to this book as you navigate into adulthood and shatter the illusions for yourself.

"Your word is a lamp for my feet, a light on my path."
Psalm 119:105

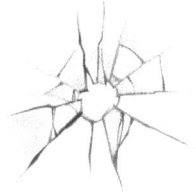

REFERENCES

Arizona Teachers Academy at ASU. (2021, February 09). Retrieved April 27, 2021, from https://education.asu.edu/arizona-teachers-academy-at-asu

Baluch, A. (2021, January 27). *What Is a Short-Term Personal Loan?* Experian. https://www.experian.com/blogs/ask-experian/what-is-a-short-term-personal-loan/.

Berlanti, G., Helbing, T., Johns, G., & Sarah Schechter. (n.d.). Pilot . *Superman & Lois*. episode, CW Network.

Bloch Chambers, S., Chrisley, T., Greener, A., & Sayer, J. (n.d.). *Chrisley Knows Best*. whole, USA Network.

CDC. Youth Risk Behavior Surveillance—United States, 2019. *MMWR Suppl* 2020;69(1):1-83

Georgia Student Finance Commission. (n.d.). Hope. Retrieved April 27, 2021, from https://gsfc.georgia.gov/hope

Indeed. (2020, November 25). Transferable skills: Definitions and examples. Retrieved March 11, 2021, from https://www.indeed.com/career-advice/resumes-cover-letters/transferable-skills

My Next Move. (n.d.). Retrieved March, 2021, from https://www.mynextmove.org/

Nichols, L. (2018, June 7). Be Perfect in Your Imperfection | Lisa Nichols | Inspiring Women of Goalcast. YouTube. https://www.youtube.com/watch?v=g8pgUGx7Pkw.

Photo Career Quiz. (n.d.). Retrieved March, 2021, from https://www.truity.com/

Starbucks College Achievement Plan. (n.d.). Go to college, on us. Retrieved April 27, 2021, from https://starbucks.asu.edu/

Steve Harvey Radio Show [Radio series episode]. (n.d.). IHeartRadio.

Washington, P. C. (2012). *Real Money Answers - College Life & Beyond*. Seek Wisdom, Find Wealth.

Wikimedia Foundation. (2021, May 20). *Life, Liberty and the pursuit of Happiness.*

Wikipedia. https://en.wikipedia.org/wiki/Life,_Liberty_and_the_pursuit_of_Happiness.

Young women of faith Bible: N.I.V., New International Version. (2001). Grand Rapids, MI: Zonderkidz.

PAMELA "PAM" SMITH was born and raised in Orlando, Florida and joined the U.S. Navy right out of high school at seventeen years old. After that, she lived another twenty years in Georgia and is now currently an Arizona resident. Pam has always been inquisitive about the world and other cultures. The military allowed her to travel while serving her country. In the first half of her career journey, she realized that she most enjoyed helping people plan out the next steps in their careers. As a successful career coach, Pam works closely with individuals to assess their needs on how to leverage their current experiences and ideas to develop new skills to advance their career. By considering additional factors such as the individual's natural talents and abilities, as well as applicable life experiences, she helps to devise a unique action plan specific to the person. All while considering employment standards and competition, Pam understands that knowledge and adequate training are the foundations of accountability. As Pam enters a new phase of her life, she is inspired by her mentors and leaders to challenge herself, and emboldened to share her knowledge and to collaborate with spiritual leaders, life coaches, and healers.

www.ingramcontent.com/pod-product-compliance
Lightning Source LLC
Chambersburg PA
CBHW071457070526
44578CB00001B/372